Australian Biographical Monographs

13

Australian Biographical Monographs
Series Editor: Scott Prasser

Previous Volumes

Australian Biographical Monographs

13

Margaret Guilfoyle

Anne Henderson

Connor Court Publishing

Published in 2021 by Connor Court Publishing Pty Ltd

Connor Court Publishing Pty Ltd
PO Box 7257
Redland Bay QLD 4165
sales@connorcourt.com
www.connorcourt.com
Phone 0497-900-685

Printed in Australia

ISBN: 9781922449801

Front cover design: Maria Giordano

Front cover picture: Getty Images

Where do you start with Margaret? She was a terrific minister. She had this calm confidence that stood her in great stead in very fraught discussions. ... We kept hearing that her colleagues respected her views and respected the fact that she stayed unruffled and got things through.

– Helen Williams AC[1]

Series overview

The Connor Court *Australian Biographical Series* focusses on on past leading Australian political leaders and other important figures seeks to provide an overview for those who are unfamiliar with the subject and to highlight the person's particular importance, controversies, and contributions to Australia's progress.

The monographs are scholarly rather than academic in focus, placing emphasis on a clear narrative, but with careful attention to referencing to ensure views expressed are supported by appropriate sources and evidence.

The Series was initiated because of the decline in the study of Australian history at our schools and universities. Consequently, there has been a lack of knowledge or, even worse, distorted views, of some of Australia's leading historical figures who deserve to be remembered, better understood for their achievements, and, as each volume also highlights, their flaws.

This is the first biography of Dame Margaret Guilfoyle, Liberal Senator from Victoria from 1971 to 1987, who quickly rose to become Minister for Social Security and then Minister for Finance in the Fraser Coalition Government. Margaret Guilfoyle had the distinction of being the first woman to hold a cabinet-level ministerial portfolio in Australia. She was regarded as an outstanding minister – highly competent, reformist, and trustworthy.

That she served as a senior minister for the duration of the Fraser Government testifies to this. In addition, Margaret Guilfoyle did much to increase women's participation and representation in Australian politics through her own outstanding example, and active roles in various forums across the political divide.

Anne Henderson is deputy director of the Sydney Institute and has been a major contributor to promoting the study of Australian politics through her many publications. Among her books of note are *Enid Lyons: Leading Lady To A Nation*; *Joseph Lyons – The People's Prime Minister*; *Menzies at War* (short listed for the 2015 Prime Minister's Award for Australian History); and *Federation's Man of Letters – Patrick McMahon Glynn*.

-- Scott Prasser

If anyone's performance should have established that a woman's place was in Cabinet, it was Margaret Guilfoyle's

– The Hon Susan Ryan AO

There is a black and white photo in the National Archives of Australia collections taken during the Fraser Government, 1976-83. As they look towards the camera, four male figures in dark or darkish suits tower over a diminutive female standing in the middle, dressed in a light suit. The contrast is remarkable. Moreover, in spite of high heels, the slightly built lady barely makes the height of her colleagues' shoulders. She is Senator Dame Margaret Guilfoyle; her parliamentary colleagues in the photo are The Hon Doug Anthony, Prime Minister Malcolm Fraser, Senator Austin Lewis and Liberal member for Hotham Roger Johnston.

In the overwhelmingly male dominated Australian parliament of the 1970s and 1980s, such workmates might have stood head and shoulders over her, but Margaret Guilfoyle as a Liberal Party senator and minister, from July 1971 until retirement in June 1987, was a presence to be reckoned with. Her command of detail, exacting work practices, professional demeanour and impeccable manners while standing her ground made her exceptional. She could reduce a bombastic head of department to compliant public servant without so much as a cross word. A tolerant hearing, along with a firm stare, would do.

An Empire lass

Superlatives aside, Margaret Guilfoyle was not raised in any sort of political atmosphere. Born in Belfast on 15 May 1926, her family migrated to Australia just over two years later. As she told historian Barry York for her interview in the Oral History Project for Old Parliament House, she might have ticked every box in a questionnaire for immigrants arriving in Australia, except for "language other than English spoken at home".[2] Her father William McCartney had been a head constable in the Royal Ulster Constabulary but either for reasons of health or the troubled state of Northern Ireland at the time (or both) he went ahead to Melbourne looking for work and soon brought his family to settle there. Margaret was under three on the sea voyage, with her brother Brian two years older. Their mother, a trained teacher, was sick for most of the voyage. A third child, Rosalie, was born not long after in Australia.

There would be no fresh start with opportunities as Elizabeth and William McCartney had hoped. A rheumatic heart, Margaret Guilfoyle recalls, seemed to be at the root of her father's long stints in hospital, at times up to ten weeks. She and her brother often visited him and retained fond memories of a loving father. When Margaret was just ten, William died leaving Elizabeth far from her relatives, a widow and with three young children to rear. Margaret remembers that her father died during Melbourne Cup week, which meant they missed their big Sunday school picnic.

Looking back after being a successful MP, Margaret Guilfoyle would muse that for all their privation, the fatherless McCartney family in Hall Street, Fairfield, opposite a park adjoining Plimsole Grove, was "rich in everything but money". They had no holidays away but entertained themselves joining the tribes of neighbourhood children in the park or at community competitive sports events and activities run by local churches. It was an era of strong community ties where many people volunteered as organisers. Guilfoyle recognised that times were a struggle for most families in the 1930s and believed theirs was a life of frugality not penury. They had a dog called Nero, numbers of cats, even a canary. There was no radio in her early years, but they all read books and their mother read to them and numbers of their neighbourhood friends or told them stories. Rosalie learnt the piano. They had little political interest as children, just civics at school that taught something of government.

The McCartney family was strictly Presbyterian with Elizabeth a leader in the local church groups, doing readings and chairing meetings. She was the great strength of the family unit, keeping her children at school as long as she could afford it. She herself had won prizes for her creative talents as a student and she valued education highly. Margaret attended Fairfield Primary school and then Westgarth Central school. Her school memories were all positive with no recollection of trauma. Teachers were dedicated people and she had loyal friends. In spite of eventually choosing accountancy for a career, it was Latin and classical history that were her great love at Westgarth Central.

A quick learner as she moved up the levels, Margaret skipped a grade. She would have loved to have gone on to university, but fees had to be paid and there were no scholarships to assist. Instead, she found employment and attended night school doing accountancy at Taylors Institute of Advanced Studies and later at the Royal Melbourne Institute of Technology. By the age of 21, Margaret McCartney would be a fully qualified accountant and chartered accountant. Former Senator Margaret Reid, looking back on the person she knew as a colleague, reflected that Guilfoyle's mother Elizabeth would have been a significant force in her daughter's ambition to succeed: "Her mother must have made it plain that what she wanted to do, she could do. She had the ability. But she never exhibited any sort of conceit about having achieved anything".[3]

Something of the politically astute figure she would become as Senator Margaret Guilfoyle is evident in how Margaret McCartney made her way in her accountancy career. Her first job was with a Japanese firm. The firm was involved in the import/export business – silks from Japan; wool from

Australia. The young Guilfoyle was suddenly thrust into a grown-up world. The company dealt with a number of other Japanese enterprises in Australia. Margaret came to know many Japanese as polite, friendly people and would retain good relations with Japanese Australians over her lifetime. It was also a fast-learning curve for a girl of fourteen among a small staff of eight. After the Japanese attack on the US base at Pearl Harbor in December 1941, the firm was closed and Australian government authorities commandeered her shorthand notebook.

War had sapped the male workforce in Australia. Young women with skills found opportunities. It was Guilfoyle's belief that the war years gave her time to develop her skills, qualifications and experience which put her ahead of male contemporaries when they resumed life back home after the war and had to be retrained at a time when accountants were scarce. In the years of Australia's Pacific war, Margaret worked for a merchandise manager at D M W Murray Limited where she was what she described as a mixture of Girl Friday and accountant. Her tasks could be anything from keeping quota figures, typing, shorthand, taking dictation to looking after company visitors and organising their travel. It was what Guilfoyle calls learning from being given a 'first chance' to develop. At all times, her focus was on outcomes. In 1946, she moved on to work for the Overseas Corporation (Australia Ltd) where she became head office accountant.

Politically engaged

It was at night school after the war that Margaret met Stan Guilfoyle. He was a member of her class. As Stan recalls it, he was not looking for a girlfriend but rather help with notetaking in class, having flown with the American Catalina Squadron during the Pacific War while a member of the RAAF. Margaret was the only woman in the class and sat a few desks in front of him. They became friends and began to meet up socially. There was the occasional dance and Margaret would watch Stan at his athletics meetings. Stan had been educated at Essendon Grammar and was active in community groups generally. It would be a couple of years before the relationship became more than friendship. From the outset, however, Stan recalls that they developed a trust in each other.[4] They married on 20 November 1952, the ceremony held in the newly built Fairfield Presbyterian church. It was the first wedding the church had hosted. Margaret's brother Brian gave her away and her sister Rosalie was bridesmaid.

The war years had not particularly affected Margaret. There was continuing concern at what was happening in Europe, especially as her family was so staunchly British. Her brother Brian had served in the RAAF and would become active in the Returned Services League in the post war years. She did, however, recall being very concerned when the Japanese advancement and the Pacific war involved Australia. At home, her family had never taken part in politics in her local electorate where Labor was dominant. And family loyalties were conservative. In December 1936, newly widowed Elizabeth McCartney cried on the abdication of the uncrowned Edward VIII. As the war years lengthened, the McCartney family believed, along with most citizens of their adopted country, that Australian forces were fighting the war under a British identity. Links with the Empire were fundamental.

This somewhat politically detached world for Margaret McCartney would all change with Stan Guilfoyle. An immigrant from England who had made the journey to Australia as a single woman, Stan's mother was politically active. She was a member of Elizabeth Couchman's Australian Women's National League (AWNL) that had been significant in the formation of the Liberal Party of Australia in 1944-45. In fact, Stan's mother had enrolled him as a foundation member of the Liberal Party when he was still in the RAAF. As momentum grew in opposition to the Chifley Government's bank nationalisation legislation, Guilfoyle remembers a general feeling of wanting change. On holidays at the time of the December 1949 election that swept the Menzies Liberals into government, Guilfoyle voted for the first time after getting a letter from her mother reminding her to vote.

Margaret Guilfoyle told Barry York for her Oral History Project that she joined the Liberal Party in 1953. Once married, Stan and Margaret had bought a house in Glen

Iris and both subsequently joined the South Camberwell branch of the Liberal Party. Previously, Stan had been a member of the Essendon branch. Margaret soon became branch secretary at South Camberwell.

The 1950s was an exciting time for Liberals as the fledgling party grew quickly and developed under the Menzies Government's leadership and as the country rebuilt after the war. Guilfoyle singled out to Barry York what she saw as the big factors in the Liberal Party's 1950s success - good and stable government and the boost given to prosperity with the 'new look' immigration program alongside the drama over the split in the Labor Party and the formation of the Democratic Labor Party (DLP) which divided Labor's vote, especially in Victoria and Queensland. Liberal Party branch meetings were lively events – politically and socially. A number of members of their branch, Stan recalls, were married couples so much so that on one occasion there was a motion to ban married couples speaking on the same motion or issue. For all that, the Guilfoyles carefully balanced their activities in their political engagement.

In later life, Margaret Guilfoyle reflected on how busy her political involvement was, right from the beginning. Stan was accustomed to community activities and at all times encouraged Margaret to be as committed to the party as he was. From the outset, Margaret was an office bearer, with Stan very soon on the state executive of the party. Meanwhile the family unit grew; daughter Georgina was born in 1956, Anne two years later and Geoff two years after that. Margaret had opened a small accountancy business of her own – this would be called working from home more than half a century on.

Liberal Party divisions over policy, as Margaret Guilfoyle saw them, were not factional except for occasional divides along state lines. Years later, she would describe her allegiance to Andrew Peacock, albeit not at leadership votes, as "because he's a Victorian".[5] She saw no structure to factionalism in the Liberal Party. Her understanding of political philosophy underpinning the Liberal Party was the belief that people/citizens must accept responsibilities. Government could not and must not take over all responsibility. Government was there to support individual effort and those needing help, with people of common purpose ready to work beside government to ensure just outcomes. In Victoria, the era of the Bolte Liberal Government influenced her thinking – policies around the development of housing, services and education.

Under the Liberal Party's rules in Victoria, fifty per cent of organisational positions must go to women – what Robert Menzies at the Albury Conference in 1944 referred to as "men and women working equally for the one body".[6] This was a progressive decision made not least as a result of Menzies' reliance on the strength in numbers of Elizabeth (May) Couchman's AWNL, an organisation so important in bringing together the disparate non-Labor forces in

1944-45 to form the Liberal Party. The AWNL with tens of thousands of members had underpinned the non-Labor side of politics for decades, particularly in Victoria. They were women who were not only politically astute but who manned voluntary organisations and knew how the community worked. Adopting the 50/50 rule, the Liberal Party in Victoria, as an organisation, gave women like Margaret Guilfoyle an opportunity to take leadership roles in the party structure and gain experience for any future political role. But it would take more than prominence in the party structure, as a woman, to actually take a seat.

On the non-Labor side of Australian politics, Elizabeth Couchman was a remarkable political force but was never given an opportunity to take a winnable seat. She failed three times to be pre-selected for the Senate – largely due to selectors' preference for male candidates. When given the nomination for the blue ribbon Labor seat of Melbourne for the 1943 election, which ended in a Labor landslide, she was defeated as expected. By 1949, aged 73, time was against her even though Couchman's potential as a candidate was never in doubt. With the unexpected success of Dame Enid Lyons in 1943, winning the seat of Darwin in northern Tasmania for the United Australia Party which became the Liberal Party, a few scales fell from preselector eyes and, at the 1949 election, Ivy Wedgewood for the Liberals in Victoria and Agnes Robertson for the Country Party in Western Australia gained seats in the Senate. Ivy Wedgewood was also a senior officeholder in the AWNL.

A founding member of the Essendon branch of the Liberal Party, as well as a long- time member of the AWNL, Ivy Wedgewood was a friend of Stan's mother. In time, she became close to Stan and Margaret. With the Guilfoyles becoming a strength of the South Camberwell branch of the party and the Liberal Party of Victoria generally, Ivy Wedgewood approached Stan to run as a Liberal candidate. He declined saying that he needed a financially secure career and a seat in parliament might not ensure that.[7] However, Margaret increasingly found herself in leadership roles within the Victorian Women's Section of the party. In 1969-70 she was chair of the Women's Section at the same time as being a member of the party's state executive and of its Federal Council. Ivy Wedgewood had meanwhile turned her attention to Margaret and had become something of a mentor. As Guilfoyle told author Margaret Fitzherbert, "During those years that I was Chairman [Women's Section] Ivy kept fairly close to me to make sure I knew what was expected and where the government was going on policy and that sort of thing".[8]

A parliamentary "first chance"

Former Senator Margaret Guilfoyle was wont to say, "I am a product of my time".[9] This brief reflection says more about Guilfoyle's modest assessment of herself – a feature of females of her generation - than it does about Guilfoyle's achievements. Journalist Terry Barnes captured her exceptional achievements in an obituary piece:

> Margaret Guilfoyle was a politician of firsts. One of the first women in the Senate. The first woman to hold a cabinet portfolio. The first woman to be minister of finance.[10]

On 29 November 2020, Australia's Treasurer, The Hon Josh Frydenberg, a good friend and the Member for Kooyong, moved the Condolence Motion in Guilfoyle's memory in the House of Representatives saying:

> She beckons us as a country, as a government, as a party and as individuals – to see this place – to see our politics – as reflective, as broad and as representative as the people we serve. She pried open those doors for everyone – for every background, every gender and every creed.[11]

These are achievements the women of Margaret Guilfoyle's time could only dream about.

Yet, there is some truth in how Guilfoyle saw herself. Not unlike Dame Enid Lyons before her, Margaret Guilfoyle did not set out on a political trajectory that was planned or pre-determined. This was no feminist with a burning desire to overthrow the status quo or even a woman with a plan for how to reach parliamentary heights. But, like Lyons, opportunities came her way – in Enid Lyons' case they could be more like hurdles – and Guilfoyle took them in her stride. She was ambitious but not in the sense that many men are, or as her male parliamentary colleagues would have been. Her ambition did not flash itself but lay within her when the chances came. Her belief in learning from "first chance" stayed with her. So it was that an opening came her way when Ivy Wedgewood announced her retirement from the Senate in 1970 and preselection began for her seat.

When it was known that Senator Ivy Wedgewood would not recontest her seat in the Senate, the Liberal Party called for nominations. It would prove to be a large field with twenty applicants for the vacancy and only three of them women. Margaret Guilfoyle, however, as Chair of the Women's Section, just as Ivy Wedgewood had been when she won the nomination for the 1949 election, was seen by many as an obvious successor to Senator Wedgewood. Guilfoyle was encouraged to put her name forward. Guilfoyle was also inspired by other strong AWNL leaders like Elizabeth Couchman and Edith Haynes. But there were further complications. Senator John Gorton, occupying what was considered a 'country position' for Victoria, had moved to the House of Representatives to become the Member for Higgins after he was elected leader of the Liberal Party and Prime Minister in December 1967. When Ivor Greenwood from Melbourne was chosen to replace Gorton, this meant a 'country' or regional position in the Senate had been lost. Candidate Margaret Guilfoyle was up against it.

Stan Guilfoyle was close to the Victorian Liberal Premier, Henry Bolte, a master of Victorian Liberal politics with a good sense of the numbers. Bolte was also hoping Wedgewood's replacement with a country candidate would help him win votes in regional Victoria. One particular country candidate had Bolte's backing and Bolte assured Stan Guilfoyle that Margaret did not have a chance. This he was certain of even though the choice of candidates had been reduced to two – Margaret Guilfoyle and Bolte's candidate. Stan imagined it was all over and his wife had no chance of winning.[12]

Stan Guilfoyle would never have stood in his wife's way but it was something of a relief to think she would not win. How would he manage if Margaret took a seat in federal parliament? She was the mainstay of their domestic scene and, professionally, only worked from home, which left the bulk of caring for three growing Guilfoyle youngsters capably in her corner. Stan, meanwhile, was working in the finance section of Hamersley Iron.

However, the question – it being 1970 and not a half century later – was on other minds as well and became part of the preselection process. At the interview stage, Margaret Guilfoyle was singled out by the Member for Latrobe, John Jess, and asked who would look after her children if she won the nomination. Her quick witted reply undoubtedly impressed selectors: "I'm asking you to make a decision to give me responsibility to be a representative in the Senate and I would ask that you would accept that I have the responsibility to make decisions regarding my family".[13] The formidable Beryl Beaurepaire, who was a delegate, was not impressed with the question. As selectors interviewed the next candidate, she upped the ante and asked who would care for his children should he become a senator. Guilfoyle won the nomination to replace Ivy Wedgewood. It was, reflected Margaret Guilfoyle, a watershed moment as from then on it became accepted that one Senate position, at least, in Victoria would be taken by a woman.

It was with some shock that the Guilfoyle family realised Margaret had won. Stan recalls they sat down at the table that night and took stock of how it would change their family life. He had been climbing in the business world but now it was Margaret's turn. They were by then living at 21 Howard Street, Studley Park Kew, just opposite Bob and Pattie Menzies' old house at 10 Howard Street. Their three children were by this time aged 14, 12 and 10. Geoff was at school at nearby Trinity Grammar and Georgina and Anne attended Ruyton, also nearby. Margaret remembers they eventually managed a backup service with some paid child minders. Stan, who was there, is more grateful for the next door neighbours and family friends that he relied on who helped with the extra hours of care. A group developed around him giving support and he learned to cook, at a basic level.

For all this, Stan Guilfoyle regrets that it was hard on their children, especially explaining to them the importance of what Margaret was doing and her need to be away, often. While parliamentary sittings were fragmented over a year, there was also electorate obligations for a senator that could require travelling the state. Now and again, there would be a bit of an outburst against Mum from the young Guilfoyles and Stan would soothe the waters. The kids "got away with murder", says Stan although that only referred to a certain lax discipline that their mother would not have tolerated. But, like many families, they managed. Stan says he became used to being "a bit of a Prince Phillip chap" – walking two steps behind his wife.[14]

Margaret Guilfoyle entered the Senate, in July 1971, having won her seat while being placed second on the Victorian Senate ticket at the half Senate election held in November 1970. Determined to play her part not as a singled-out female but as a person like any male, ironically Guilfoyle would spend her career noted in the press as just that – the female MP – with maternal and homely metaphors grabbing many of the headlines she made. On her preselection, John Larkin began the typecasting with an article headed "A Liberal Lady with open doors on her mind". In spite of quoting Guilfoyle's strong assertion that she wanted to be elected "to represent the whole of Victoria not just the women" and that she had never seen herself as taking "any lesser responsibility than a man doing the same job", Larkin went on to write that her "confidence as a woman dealing with men comes from being an accountant".[15]

Settling into parliamentary life is a bit like being a boarder starting at a new school. There are written and unwritten rules and procedures that cannot be ignored - most to be learnt as you go. Margaret Guilfoyle enjoyed her first day with Magnus Cormack from Victoria being elected the Senate's new President. A Victorian, Cormack was a close friend of Stan and Margaret Guilfoyle. And, in the Liberal Party, colleagues from one's home state are often one's closest colleagues. David Kemp, adviser to Malcolm Fraser and former Member for Goldstein in Victoria, notes that federal Liberal Party MPs at the time conducted their politics largely from their state base: "The amount of politics that went on interstate was only that which was necessary to deal with issues that came up within the federal area ... generally speaking the politics went on within the states and states didn't know a lot about each other and their internal politics".[16]

With the opening of parliament, the whole Guilfoyle family attended; it was a proud moment in a big new step. Old Parliament House was not unfamiliar to Guilfoyle as she had been there for committee meetings over the years. John Gorton was no longer Prime Minister as Margaret Guilfoyle took her seat in the Senate. His term of office had ended in a party room meeting following the resignation of Malcolm Fraser as Minister for Defence, in March 1971. Fraser had announced his resignation in parliament saying Gorton was "not fit to hold the great office of prime minister".[17] There had been continuing party instability and unrest over Gorton's performance, which began after the government had come close to losing the October 1969 federal election. When the vote of confidence at the party meeting was tied, Gorton announced it was no vote of confidence and had resigned. The party room, suddenly needing a new leader, then elected Treasurer William McMahon to become party leader and Prime Minister. The other contender, Billy Snedden, later claimed the vote was close.[18]

It was the tail end of a long Liberal Party era of dominance since 1949. But with the retirement of Sir Robert Menzies in 1966, the sudden drowning of his popular successor Harold Holt at Portsea Beach in late 1967 and the re-energised and more united Labor Party with its new leader Gough Whitlam, who took the Labor leadership in February 1967, a shift was at play in political fortunes. Guilfoyle recalled 1972 as a very difficult year for the Liberals and her parliamentary colleagues. Their leader McMahon, whatever his political savvy at the party level, lacked charisma and was easily mocked. Looking back, Guilfoyle reflected a disappointment that John Gorton had been toppled.[19]

Meanwhile, on the ground, the new Senator Guilfoyle had

a lot to learn. Stan pointed out to his wife that while she had mastered political skills within the party organisation, this was secretarial experience not policy experience. He advised her not to take on any responsibilities or portfolios that were women's issues. If she was to make it, she should make it as a person like any man. He suggested she take opportunities in finance or administration. The advice was taken.

A list of the parliamentary committees Guilfoyle accepted show that she was keen to demonstrate her capability with finance but also that she had an interest in joint party co-operation. Recalling her early work in the Senate, Guilfoyle told Barry York that the Senate provided excellent opportunities to work with MPs from other parties such as the DLP senators who were significant in support for the government. Guilfoyle joined the Senate Standing Committee on Finance and Government Operations as well as the Public Accounts Committee. The former, with its opportunities to travel Australia, she regarded as a unique learning curve and a chance to gain experience in affairs of foreign investment and industries such as mining. Guilfoyle also served on estimates committees. She regarded Senator Ivor Greenwood highly and Senator John Marriott from Tasmania taught her how to have questions ready from reading reports.

Margaret Guilfoyle's first speech in the Senate was made on Wednesday 15 September 1971. It was a wide-ranging speech, in support of the government's 1971-72 Budget. From a perspective of half a century on, it is also a speech that holds its own, giving voice to the contribution the Australian mining industry was making to infrastructure, with little government outlay or support. A contribution that continues even more so in the world of 2021. Mining, Senator Guilfoyle argued, invested in port development, railways, airstrips, off-mine roads, power and water services and paid rates to local councils; it was responsible for the building of towns, all constructed to government regulations, and provided housing, hospitals, shopping centres and services for not inconsiderable populations. Her other areas of interest in the speech were conservation, the environment and the arts.

Just one other female sat in the Senate in mid-1971 – Liberal Senator Nancy Buttfield – and for three months Buttfield was away at the United Nations so Margaret Guilfoyle became very used to often being the sole woman in the Senate. Facilities at Old Parliament House were well behind in catering for female MPs. Guilfoyle soon learned not to use the "Senators' Toilet" but to always head for the staff facilities. Services were also limited and the Parliament was located at a distance far from any sort of regular shopping district. There was a hairdresser but not much else.

Former Senator Kay Patterson, who would take Margaret Guilfoyle's Senate seat when she retired in 1987, looks back on how lonely it might have been for Guilfoyle. After the 1987 double dissolution, the Liberal-National Party Coalition in opposition had eight women senators – one from every state and the ACT. Labor had five and the Democrats one. Patterson gained from the support of her female colleagues in the Senate, mentoring and even simply the occasional mobile message of support after a speech from those ahead of her such as Margaret Reid and Jocelyn Newman, and the companionship of other women on her side of politics.[20]

Being an isolated female, however, seemed not to deter Senator Guilfoyle who believed MPs were there to work not recreate. Her work ethic never wavered. Anne-Marie Kemp, who worked for Guilfoyle for most of the years 1977-87, recalls how the parliament sitting times could go long, even into the early hours of the morning: "She would be working hard at 2.00 am, looking marvellous, not tired or anything. We often worked those long hours and a couple of MPs died at the time. Later, they cut the hours back".[21] Guilfoyle, like Senator Margaret Reid in time, never went to the Members Bar much less the Non-Members bar, described by Canberra journalist Rob Chalmers as "the social centre for all who worked in the place, including the parliamentarians".[22] He added, re MPs: "They had their own bar but often preferred the company available – particularly female – in the non-members bar".[23] Guilfoyle's male colleagues were little affected by a new woman among them. They were by then used to the occasional female senator. Dorothy Tangney had set a high standard from 1943. Guilfoyle found her Senate colleagues accepted her as an MP like any other. They were never embarrassed or awkward. After the double dissolution of 1974, Liberal Senator Kathy Martin from Queensland joined Guilfoyle, as well as Ruth Coleman a Labor Senator from South Australia. Nancy Buttfield had retired.

Old Parliament House was a far cosier arrangement for MPs than the vast expanse of the later 'new' Parliament House or Capital Hill where Australia's parliament has sat from 1988. At first, Guilfoyle had just one secretarial assistant who worked mostly in Melbourne, at the Senator's office in Treasury Place. As a minister, her staff allocation increased to around six. The Old Parliament was in walking distance from the Hotel Canberra or Hotel Kurrajong where many MPs stayed during sitting weeks. Later, after the Hotel Canberra closed, MPs who stayed at the Lakeside Hotel or Canberra Rex were offered a shuttle bus to the parliament. For Margaret Guilfoyle, it was a nice way to start the day. Later, when a minister, the Guilfoyles bought a two bedroomed house in Red Hill for Margaret to use. Rod Kemp who worked as Guilfoyle's chief of staff for many years from 1976 recalls staying there with his family during occasional school holidays. Guilfoyle was a generous host, the house in immaculate order.[24]

As the working week ended, Rod Kemp was grateful that Guilfoyle was never interested in socialising:

I had young children at that stage, so as a staffer it was ideal for me because as soon as we could get out of Canberra, we were on a plane and back to Melbourne ... She was very keen to get home and when parliament got up in the evening, she was straight up. A lot of politicians, myself even, tend to mix with colleagues, go for a drink or something but she, as soon as the bells went, she was off.[25]

Guilfoyle, however, was not without good friends. Her work in the party gave her strong bonds with colleagues, especially those from Melbourne. Former MP and Senator Michael Baume had a feeling Guilfoyle was a Gorton admirer. Even so, she was a loyal Fraser team player in her years as a minister. Enjoying a meal on one occasion with parliamentary colleagues in the Members' Dining Room, she was asked if they were plotting a coup. It was simply that they were celebrating the fact that they all had birthdays on the same day.

Rod Kemp noted that Guilfoyle was a friendly person whom people liked. She had warm relations with parliamentarians in other parties. She was not a drinker and Rod Kemp noticed that at social functions Guilfoyle would keep a glass of white wine in her hand so as not to be asked for refills. "She had a number of stratagems," says Rod Kemp, "Labor people seemed to like her too. She was someone you went to for advice. ... She was quite atypical in many ways".[26] None of which stopped gossip. In 1976, Guilfolye's particular friendship with her colleague Jim

Killen, then Minister for Defence, saw a gossipy piece in the leftist *Nation Review* alleging there was more to it. The allegation was strongly denied and ended in court, with Killen and Guilfoyle winning an injunction against any further public comment.[27]

Opposition and 1975

Labor's defeat of the Coalition government in December 1972 was no landslide but it left the Liberal-Country Party Coalition in disarray. An era of ascendency was over – even if the signs of it had been there for some time. Change, even revolutionary change, was about to happen. The phrase "crash through or crash" would become the Whitlam Government's hallmark. Yet, with a major list of reforms to be enacted, the Whitlam Government was hampered by a Senate where it did not have a majority. In May 1974, a double dissolution election returned the Whitlam Government to office and saw the passing of reform legislation in a Joint House sitting. But the election had resulted in the Whitlam Government still being left without an outright majority in the Senate and needing the vote of Tasmanian independent Michael Townley (who in early 1975 joined the Liberals) and/or National Alliance Senator Tom Drake-Brockman (who sat with the Country Party) to pass legislation if Coalition senators opposed it. It was not the outcome Prime Minister Whitlam had hoped for.

In March 1975, Malcolm Fraser rolled Liberal leader Billy Snedden and took over as Opposition leader – the Liberal Party had now had six leaders in just over eight years. Malcolm Fraser was a new breed of Liberal leader, committed to strong conservative principles, commanding and effective in the media. His lack of popularity with the chattering classes was no drawback in the suburbs and regional areas. Meanwhile, the effect of inflation and growing unemployment figures had introduced a new word into the political lexicon – stagflation. To this was added the inexperience of the Labor team as skyrocketing expenditure became matched by erratic personalities and scandal. As a young Treasury officer, Helen Williams recalls how Jim Cairns as Treasurer, from December 1974 until July 1975, seemed to be uninterested in the detail that the department required. "We were sitting around trying to find things to do because he simply wasn't interested".[28] Only when Cairns was replaced by Bill Hayden, did Williams see serious work on an incomes review begin, work which eventually impacted on the new family allowance brought in under Guilfoyle as Social Security Minister in the Fraser Government.

For Margaret Guilfoyle, looking back on 1975 with Barry York, the drama of November 1975 and Governor-General Sir John Kerr's dismissal of Prime Minister Gough Whitlam was only the climax of a very long year. From the time of Malcolm Fraser's election as leader, discussions about how to deal with the Whitlam Government's legislation were ongoing. The Opposition by then had the numbers in the Senate to delay or defeat important government legislation but differing opinions were at play. An opposition blocking legislation in the Senate could be unpopular and seen as obstructive to good government. Then the Loans Affair broke – a scandal involving the Whitlam Government seeking to borrow a huge amount of money to finance its spending through an intermediary Pakistani banker named Tirath Khemlani. The matter was highly irregular and threatened relations with the United States, among others. As uproar in the media increased, the Opposition saw a chance to bring down, by late 1975, a very unpopular government.

In October 1975, the Liberal-Country Party Opposition used its numbers in the Senate to defer the passing of the Whitlam Government's Appropriation Bills, which financed government expenditure. It was the beginning of the gridlock that would culminate in the Dismissal (as it would become known) on 11 November. Inside the Coalition, the political heat being put on the government required team loyalty and rock solid unity. At least one senator – Victorian Alan Missen – was uncertain of the propriety of blocking supply. South Australian Senator Don Jessop was another who was inclined to waver.

Guilfoyle had no misgivings about the plan to block supply. Paul Kelly's *November 1975 – The Inside Story of Australia's Greatest Political Crisis* gives a forensic analysis of the tensions and close-run operation the drama in Canberra of November 1975 was within the Liberal Party with Reg Withers, Opposition leader in the Senate, and Malcolm Fraser playing a poker game in politics. Whitlam would not bend and hold a general election, supply would run out if the Appropriation Bills were defeated in the Senate and Malcolm Fraser was not letting Whitlam win the day. Years later, Margaret Guilfoyle summed up the state of play: "It was very difficult for Reg Withers. Any speculation about how much longer it could have held is really just speculation. Withers held them long enough for Kerr to be satisfied and that's what mattered".[29] In an interview for Kelly's book, Reg Withers told him, "[W]e had some people who were great strengths – Ivor Greenwood, Harold Young, Margaret Guilfoyle and Kathy Martin [later Sullivan]".[30]

In the Senate, Guilfoyle argued the Opposition case strongly in a reply to Labor Senator George Georges on 5 November 1975:

> *Suffice it is to say at this stage that the Opposition is using the mechanism of the Constitution to force the Government to an election by the people of Australia. It is doing this not by dealing with Bills at this stage but by using the Budget Bills as the means for endeavouring to ensure that the people of Australia are given the opportunity to vote on the continuation of this Government which has acted in an unconstitutional manner in a variety of ways.... It is on this basis that we believe that personal and corporate confidence will not be engendered until there is a change of government*

> with the object of introducing many of the excellent
> recommendations in the Mathews report [on inflation and
> taxation].

In Kelly's *November 1975*, he relates that Withers recalled Margaret Guilfoyle making an aside after Sir John Kerr opined at their swearing in how he knew they would never crack and that he had to act to end the stalemate. The particular aside was not recalled by Guilfoyle when speaking to Kelly but she did admit that, "If I did make any comment it would have been referring to Withers' difficulties in holding together such a precarious margin".[31]

The saga that became November 1975 has been written and talked about endlessly, become TV drama and more besides. Throughout the morning of 11 November, the day of Whitlam's dismissal, the game continued after he was dismissed. Gough Whitlam went home to the Lodge for lunch while Malcolm Fraser briefed his colleagues. The Opposition, by then the new caretaker government, planned to pass the Appropriation Bills in the Senate that afternoon. Whitlam, however, did not brief his colleagues. Margaret Guilfoyle, recalled meeting Labor Senator Jim McClelland in King's Hall on the day and, as she told me for my book *Getting Even – Women MPs on Life, Power and Politics*:

> He said to me, "Margaret, tell me, is it just Whitlam
> or all of us?" I said, "No, you're all gone." And he
> said, "Oh." He didn't know. And McClelland was in
> Cabinet.[32]

Margaret Guilfoyle

What followed was possibly the most acrimonious election campaign in Australian history. In this double dissolution election campaign, held 18 months after the double dissolution of 1974, Gough Whitlam, enraged at being robbed of government by a Governor-General, spoke at rallies of howling supporters while the caretaker Prime Minister, Malcolm Fraser, campaigned on the need for an end to a tumultuous three years under Labor. The result on election day 13 December was a landslide for the Coalition. In Margaret Guilfoyle's view it was a sign that Fraser had been right – the people wanted an election and a change of government. That support for the Coalition, recalled Guilfoyle, continued well past the next election.

In 1974, Opposition leader Billy Snedden had given Margaret Guilfoyle responsibility for the media. When Malcolm Fraser took the leadership, he made Guilfoyle the Opposition spokesman on education. At the time, future premier of Victoria Joan Kirner was president of the Australian Council of State Schools Organisation (ACSSO) and a strong opponent of Coalition funding for non-government schools. In spite of this, Kirner told *The Age* after the announcement that Guilfoyle would move to Social Security that government school parents would be disappointed. Guilfoyle, Kirner said, had been the architect of Coalition education policy which "under her competent guidance the Liberal-NCP recognises for the first time its national responsibility to promise equality of opportunity and community participation in schools".[33]

Big spender

As 1976 opened, Guilfoyle found herself not only the first woman in Australian politics to hold a cabinet portfolio, as Minister for Social Security, but a minister who would be responsible for one of the biggest budgets in government. As she herself described it in an article for the *Canberra Bulletin of Public Administration* in August 1995:

> As a large-spending minister, as I was going into a government, following a short period of Labor Government, with the objective of restraining the growth of government expenditure, it was not an easy task to undertake. For some periods, particularly in the initial review of expenditure, it was a case of trying to maintain and not dislocate a social security system that had been developed by successive governments over the entire post-war period.[34]

In a paper given as an address to The Sydney Institute in January 2014, economist John O'Mahony made a balanced assessment of the three years of Labor government 1972-75. There were global financial upsets at the time that all Western economies were suffering. And, in spite of the disturbing rate of inflation and unemployment figures, Australia would not witness unemployment levels as high as those in the United States (US). That, however, did not excuse the Whitlam Government, which had forced up wages, in turn sending inflation spiraling. In September 1974, as the Budget was handed down, unemployment numbers had increased by over 50 per cent in just two months while inflation sat at 14.4 per cent. O'Mahony concluded:

> The three years of the Whitlam Government saw the economic growth rate halve, unemployment double and inflation triple. If simplistic comparisons with previous economic conditions were fair, they would be an indictment of the Labor government. And yet, despite the limitations of such approaches it is likely that common perceptions of the Labor government's economic failure are based to a significant extent on how things got worse once Gough Whitlam became prime minister.[35]

The smooth moves of public service heads of department to accommodate themselves to a new conservative regime, committed to winding back extravagant expenditure, was swift. John Menadue, as head of the Department of Prime Minister and Cabinet made his move to the new caretaker Prime Minister at lunch time on 11 November 1975, leaving the newly sacked Gough Whitlam to eat his steak alone.[36] Menadue took a car from the Lodge to Parliament House to wait upon newly appointed Malcolm Fraser, in true Sir Humphrey Appleby style. As the new government took shape in 1976, even ministers with reservations about departmental officers who had served the sacked and chaotic Labor government came to respect the professionalism of the public servants they worked with. In this, Margaret Guilfoyle was a standout for her close collaboration with the senor public servant advisers in her departments.

For all that, Guilfoyle was no slave to the advice of departmental heads. In this, former colleague in the Senate Michael Baume credited Guilfoyle's pre-parliamentary experience as crucial:

> Despite all the emphasis on her being a woman in obituaries celebrating her life, Dame Margaret Guilfoyle never played the women's card, according to her colleague Tony Staley. Gender was clearly not the most important feature of Guilfoyle's notable success as a politician. In addition to her intelligence, professional skills, strong will, compassion and common sense, a key lies in her having had real-life experience before entering parliament at 45 – as I did ... As a consequence, as her boss Malcolm Fraser said, in her several successful senior ministerial roles "She was not a captive of the bureaucracy".[37]

While no captive, Guilfoyle worked closely with her senior bureaucrats. She respected their expertise and took their advice, which she also routinely scrutinised for herself. Those with whom she worked in the bureaucracy, when contacted for this booklet, could not speak highly enough of Margaret Guilfoyle – her directness, no nonsense approach, her professionalism and her trust in her advisers. Helen Williams chuckles at Guilfoyle's occasional sharp wit, especially her comment on one officer who muddled her arguments. After one episode, Guilfoyle said to Williams, "Well Helen, she'd be really out of her depth wherever she stood in the river".[38]

Those who worked with Guilfoyle recognised her deftness at handling questions: "She didn't push herself forward but if she was asked a question, she always had an answer and she was always well prepared," says her long-time assistant Anne Marie Kemp.[39] David Stanton talked of how a handful of her departmental advisers invented what they called her 'handbag statistics' – a notebook she could carry at all times with relevant figures to whip out as needed.[40] Andrew Podger, a branch head who worked closely with Guilfoyle in Social Security and Finance, observed:

> She's still my favourite minister that I ever worked for. The group of us advising – David Stanton, Col McAlister, Helen Williams – all were very fond of her. She was a very genuine person, very interested in listening to the bureaucratic advice, which doesn't mean she always agreed with it by any means but she was a close listener to the advice.[41]

Guilfoyle told *The Bulletin* journalist Jacqueline Rees that she had been surprised not to keep the Education portfolio after the 1975 election but saw her new responsibilities in the Social Security Department as "a related area of social development".[42] She noted that as Social Security Minister she sat "on most cabinet committees dealing with economics" and that pleased her. By the time Rees' article appeared in *The Bulletin*, the Fraser Government had begun a war on 'dole bludgers', whom it saw as a factor underpinning the large unemployment figures. This had left Guilfoyle with the nickname, the 'iron butterfly'. To Rees, Guilfoyle noted that school leavers at the end of the previous year had been instructed how to lodge unemployment forms. "To take that as a starting point of a working career is very dangerous," Guilfoyle said, "It is cultivating a dependency from the beginning".[43]

However, in the year to come, there would be surprises in Cabinet as Guilfoyle fought off attempts to cut her department's outlays and funding for pensioners and parental assistance. As Rees previewed it: "Her [Guilfoyle's] attitude to changed spending on welfare mainly involves a redistribution of the dollar rather than increasing or slashing it".[44]

Margaret Guilfoyle meant what she said when opining that she was interested in public administration. Outcomes were her goal. In the first year of the Fraser Government, Guilfoyle got to work. At a time of high unemployment and inflation, the question of poverty had become a serious study. Professor Ronald Henderson of the Melbourne Institute had conducted a Poverty Inquiry initiated by the McMahon Government in 1972 and extended by the Whitlam Government.

In 1976, the Fraser Government established its own Income Security Review which David Stanton from the Social Security Department, who worked closely with Margaret Guilfoyle, believes did good work although nothing of its findings were ever published. As Treasurer, Bill Hayden had started to look at ways to reform social benefits for families. Work in the Department of Social Security had been done on answers to improving family assistance – for decades, there were child endowment payments going to mothers but these could be increased if tax rebates for dependent children, which mostly went to fathers as the single breadwinner, were cashed out and the funding moved to an increase in allowances (child endowment) for children. Moreover, tax rebates benefited the better off while those below the poverty line or near to it got nothing. Andrew Podger, at the time working with the Prime Minister's Department, saw it at close quarters:

> The Review was a group in the Prime Minister's Department supported by a parliamentary committee, including the Social Security Department. The reports from the Review went to the Cabinet. Hopefully they involved Margaret Guilfoyle closely because it all had to do with family payments, pensions and benefits. We were also closely involved in recommending the change from child endowment to family allowances. And, while the proposal came out of the Income Security Review, it was strongly supported by Margaret Guilfoyle and her department against the Treasury. The Treasury were firmly against it, while the Prime Minister's Department and Social Security were very strongly in favour.[45]

The big change to family allowances owed much to the work done by the department. As journalist Anne Summers has described it, the proposal was "the brain child" of departmental officers Colin McAlister and Ian Castles.[46] But it also won out, as Andrew Podger notes, with the support of the Prime Minister. This support, however, was not won lightly.

In a "Profile" piece in *The Australian*[47], the battle to save family allowances in the 1979 Budget was accepted as being spear headed by Guilfoyle who warned the Prime Minister that he would be heavily criticised in the media if they were cut in any attempt to make big savings. The "Profile" article described a concerned PM calling Guilfoyle, Lynch and Howard to his office where the afternoon newspapers were spread across his desk. He was being castigated as the mean leader slashing pensions – this for a Prime Minister, as the article put it, "anxious to be seen as the provider of assistance to the aged and the infirm".[48]

Guilfoyle argued that she had warned Fraser of that very possibility and he should deny it immediately or it would become a more widespread saga. Fraser agreed to kill the story. However, on his way out of Canberra, Fraser was not questioned on the Budget. So, Guilfoyle gave the words of the statement agreed to at the meeting in the Prime Minister's office to *The Sun-Herald*, "thus coolly locking up $7000 million in welfare payments for the forthcoming Budget".[49] The media onslaught undoubtedly had its effect. Yet Fraser seemed to be of two minds where savings might be made. Former Prime Minister John Howard believes that Fraser might have been persuaded in support of family allowances by the National Civic Council's B A Santamaria who was of significant influence with former DLP voters.

Social Security reform was a clear winner in any assessment of the Fraser years. David Stanton, who had worked with Guilfoyle in the Department of Social Security but speaking as an Associate Professor in the Crawford School of Public Policy at the Australian National University, looks back and regards Margaret Guilfoyle as pivotal in social service reforms during the Fraser Government. "I talk to my students about this," says Stanton. "A lot of people think only Labor is responsible for changes in social policy. The Fraser Government's changes to social policy were very significant to the social security system: universal family allowances, automatic indexation of most pensions, a supporting parent's benefit and extending that to fathers, these were all big reforms."[50]

Former Senator Rod Kemp was Guilfoyle's Senior Private Secretary for most of her time as minister. He had been working at Hamersley Iron in 1976 with Stan Guilfoyle who asked him if he could recommend names to Margaret for a chief of staff. Rod told Stan he had a shortlist of one and soon found himself in the role. Like others who worked with Guilfoyle, Rod Kemp could not speak highly enough of her. "She was a friendly person and people seemed to like her," says Rod. "But she didn't do a lot of glad-handing that so many politicians do. I found her good to work for. Working for Guilfoyle was an excellent apprenticeship for a person interested in politics".[51]

When it came to managing divisions over policy and departmental advice, Kemp says Guilfoyle was "a natural". She was a conservative person politically, but he did not see her as "impassioned", adding "she was a very practical person".[52] As to surviving the rough and tumble of political life, Rod Kemp saw Guilfoyle as being able to adjust to whatever circumstances she found herself facing. At times, he noticed Fraser would use her to fight policy battles.[53] And she did not flinch when asked to do so – even when sometimes she might then be told to step back. John Howard, who worked with her as Treasurer, remembers Guilfoyle as being able to mount a case very well – on the one hand she could make what he calls a conventional Treasury case against spending but could also stand her ground on the need to maintain welfare benefits in the interests of social justice.[54] She was conservative, but old fashioned not neo.

Despite the landslide win of December 1975, the Fraser years were increasingly disturbed by ripples of concern. Don Chipp was left out of Fraser's ministry in December 1975 and became disgruntled eventually resigning from the Liberal Party in March 1977 and going on to form a new party named the Australian Democrats. The Senate, so important in November 1975, continued to assert its strength with threats from groups of Coalition senators to cross the floor and bring down legislation. And the chattering classes in the print media stirred relentlessly at the sacking of Gough Whitlam – a distraction rather than a realistic assessment of political opinion generally. Headlines accentuated rocky times but as the results of the 1977 election showed, the average voter did not want to return to a Whitlam Government.

Much of the uncertainty on the Coalition side lay with Fraser who seemed never to have been secure in his 1975 win. In spite of having a majority in the Senate that prime ministers long after would crave, from the time of the Coalition senators' revolt over cutting the $40 funeral payment to pensioners in April 1976 Fraser became wary of losing the numbers, even more so at the polls. In time, reluctance to take a stand, with such a huge majority and for the sake of reform, would haunt the legacy of the Fraser years. The problem, according to commentator Gerard Henderson who worked as a ministerial adviser in the Fraser Government, was that not only was Malcolm Fraser "really a bit of a bleeding heart" but that, in Fraser's election policy speech of 1975, the Liberals had encouraged "expectations which no contemporary government could meet".[55]

This insecurity in the Fraser period played to Guilfoyle's advantage. The Senate continued to work on occasion as if it was a separate hand of government, one that was tasked with reviewing government legislation in its own way. Guilfoyle understood this well. Her arguments in support of her proposals often came with warnings that the Senate might object to particular measures. This was particularly so after she had been left defending the decision to cut pensioner funeral benefits while Fraser was caving into the rebel senators behind her back, in the run up to the 1976 mini-Budget.[56] It was something that journalists picked up on over time. Canberra Press Gallery journalist Peter Bowers commented: "Her [Guilfoyle's] great strength is that most of her Cabinet colleagues, including Mr Fraser, are scared stiff of her support on the backbench particularly among senators where the slightest hint on welfare cuts brings an immediate threat of revolt".[57]

On 27 March 1977, *The Sun-Herald* reported Guilfoyle's "strongly worded letter to the Prime Minister, Mr Fraser, and Treasurer, Mr Lynch, opposing any Budget cuts in social welfare programs ... She hinted strongly in her letter that the Government could face a revolt in the Senate if it tried to trim welfare payments". The letter reminded the Prime Minister and the Treasurer of the Senate revolt over the attempt to cut pensioners' funeral benefits a year before. Margaret Guilfoyle, while never openly disloyal to her leader, could mount quite a political campaign for the underdog. In another piece, Peter Bowers wrote, "Last year, Mr Lynch complained to Mr Fraser that Senator Guilfoyle was the only minister who had refused to identify departmental spending areas which could be cut".[58] The Bowers' article was about Guilfoyle's victory over Treasury concerning income testing of family allowances and tax allowances for the disabled. Bowers continued:

> It would be mischievously false to suggest that Senator Guilfoyle had any part in organising the threatened backbench revolt over the tax measures. ... The backbench did not have to be organised on this issue ... The nine or 10 Senators and up to 14 MPs prepared to cross the floor to defeat the measures were well aware of Senator Guilfoyle's stand.[59]

During the early Fraser years, Guilfoyle's relationship with her Victorian colleague and Treasurer, Phil Lynch, was strained. From the beginning of the Fraser Government, the Treasurer was facing expectations that the new government would restore financial stability, rein in government spending and reduce unemployment but the answers to the problem of wages growth, inflation, business slowdown and unemployment were not apparent to administrators in the 1970s. That would only come in the future when economists and political analysts were able to argue the need for industrial relations reform, enterprise bargaining and market driven economics. That was a battle that took years. As Russell Schneider has concluded: "Fraser sought to honour his promises to cut government spending. He proved himself to be a trimmer rather than a butcher".[60]

So it was that Margaret Guilfoyle, while Social Security Minister, played her cards and delivered. Margaret

Fitzherbert records Malcolm Fraser's observations on Guilfoyle: "She never came and grumbled about Phillip [Lynch] but I knew the relationship wasn't good. She probably would have thought he wasn't listening to reason or to argument".[61] It was Guilfoyle's recollection that she always had Fraser's support. As she told Margaret Fitzherbert, "I respected his ability, authority and experience but I think he gave me every opportunity to do what I had to do".[62] Brian Buckley believes Guilfoyle, along with Andrew Peacock and Jim Killen, was never close to Fraser.[63] But Guilfoyle could win an argument, especially if it involved accounting figures, even while her loyalty to the Prime Minister was never in question. She also believed Fraser's rural experience gave him an understanding "that a community needs support in a whole lot of ways".[64] Just as she understood this from her early experience at home with a mother as sole parent making do with little support.

That Guilfoyle style

Those who knew and worked with Margaret Guilfoyle recognised her ability not only with numbers but also her speed at scrutinising a briefing or policy document and quickly pulling out the essential parts. Most days Rod Kemp would give Guilfoyle a pile of letters drafted by the department for her signature. Many would contain standard paragraphs dealing with a particular issue. She would quickly run through them, on occasions handing one back saying, "The Department changed a paragraph there Rod, could you check it for me".[65]

During Cabinet meetings, John Howard observed that a staffer might come to her with a document to check and she would go through it quickly and give a yes or no response. "She didn't muck around. And she never seemed to get into trouble with questions when they were asked," he says.[66] Scott Prasser remembers, when he was working as a ministerial adviser in Parliament House, that his minister needed to brief Guilfoyle on a particular matter that might come up in Question Time that day. Catching her with minutes to go before the House resumed sitting, Prasser handed Guilfoyle the advice. It involved the first question she was asked and Prasser said she handled it perfectly.

Rod Kemp watched this happen on a number of occasions. As a Minister and Senator, Guilfoyle would be tasked with answering questions about other portfolios where the Minister responsible sat in the House of Representatives. These involved matters where an opposition could needle a government through a spokesperson not used to handling the area. Kemp admired Guilfoyle's tactic: "I used to prepare all her papers for Question Time and she would drive the Labor Party mad because she would always just say, 'My advice from the minister on this matter is...' and then she would just read out the response." The responses were simply the basic facts, no more, no less. Her opponents would call her a postbox and she would reply, "That's right, Rod, I'm a postbox and I'm not going to intrude into areas which are not my responsibility".[67]

But brevity and a short riposte to put a questioner from the Opposition in his place were not beyond Senator Guilfoyle either. In May 1982, as Hansard records:

> Senator Colston asked the Minister for Finance, upon notice 5 May 1982:
>
>> Are counter staff of the Minister's Department permitted to smoke whilst interviewing clients?
>>
>> Senator Dame Margaret Guilfoyle – The answer to the honourable senator's question is as follows: Over-the-counter business in my Department is minimal but I am advised that when staff is so engaged it is usual practice to refrain from smoking.

Behind the scenes, Guilfoyle was the ultimate pragmatist. Michael Baume when representing the seat of Macarthur, 1975-83, had backed a number of integrated retirement villages for federal funding in his electorate. In the Budget, Baume was upset that funding had not been allocated and went to Guilfoyle to be advised that the department had assessed the application using census figures from six years earlier. Baume made his case in a robust manner, pointing out the area he represented was part coastal and took in increasing numbers of retirees. Guilfoyle was persuaded and admitted the department was wrong. She offered to check allocations of Budget funding for any unallocated money. Make sure the projects are shovel ready, was Guilfoye's advice. Baume had no worries of that and by May the projects had the money.[68]

Marie Coleman, who worked with Guilfoyle as head of Childcare, relates a story of getting funding for women's refuges. Guilfoyle, says Coleman, never positioned herself as a radical feminist, but was "in every way a feminist".[69] It began with a late-night phone call to Coleman from Guilfoyle's office requesting a proposal for women's refuges' assistance by 8am the next morning. The refuges were crying out for funding for childcare at the time and a delegation of mothers and children were in Canberra to see the Minister for Health, Ralph Hunt. Guilfoyle had taken control. Again, it was a case of Guilfoyle reviewing what funding had yet to be allocated with the result that existing women's refuges received $10,000 each. A lot of money in the late 1970s. To break the news, Guilfoyle and Coleman met with the mothers and their clutch of children in a committee room – pencils and paper, biscuits and milk. Guilfoyle then sent them off with Coleman. When Coleman asked if they should wait for Minister Hunt, Guilfoyle told her, "No, no, I'll deal with Ralph".[70]

In a keynote address at the Australian Womenspeak

Conference in Canberra on 31 March 2003, Margaret Guilfoyle recalled a statistic given to her when Minister for Social Security. Of the payments made through the department, 83 per cent of them went to women. Considerable numbers of children were also beneficiaries.[71] Marie Coleman came to know Margaret Guilfoyle in the Senate while she was working as head of the Social Welfare Commission. During the Whitlam era, Coleman was intensely annoyed by some of the suggestions made in discussions over Whitlam's National Compensation Scheme, particularly in relation to the anomalies in it for widows and dependent children. There were meetings of heads of departments and commissions in the Cabinet room and on one occasion she found herself at loggerheads with the Prime Minister himself over what Coleman regarded as "the most economically illiterate thing I had heard". Whitlam had returned fire saying, "Gentlemen, you're all here until Mrs Coleman comes to her senses." At the airport later that day Coleman told Guilfoyle of the scene. Guilfoyle replied, "Look, my dear, that was very brave of you but really we weren't going to let it through the Senate".[72]

When Minister for Social Security, Guilfoyle offered Coleman the position of Director of the Office of Childcare which she accepted. They worked closely together thereafter. Occasionally Guilfoyle and Rod Kemp would join Marie and her partner at Coleman's house for dinner. It was a professional and a social relationship. As senior women in a man's domain, they bonded while doing good work. Coleman recalls Guilfoyle could also download on occasions, albeit in a restrained way:

> She came over to have lunch with me one day at the Lobby restaurant. She had just come out of Cabinet and she had that look I recognised, like when I am savage about something – all the muscles up the back of my neck go tight. She had that. I recognised the symptoms. So I said, "A difficult Cabinet?" She said, "The thing is," her jaw going very firm, "there are some very stupid men around but you have to keep on paddling under the water".[73]

Rod Kemp cannot think of any occasion where Margaret Guilfoyle ever lost her temper, however strained her patience might have been. This was so even with the appointment of the energetic and often eccentric Patrick Lanigan as head of the Department of Social Security. Brought over from Treasury at a time when feelings ran high that there was evidence of extensive misuse of benefits, Lanigan was a new broom with a lot of sweeping to do. Sue Pidgeon for the *Australian Dictionary of Biography* credits Lanigan with "improving efficiency in processing welfare payments and in detecting fraud".[74] Guilfoyle and Lanigan were chalk and cheese in character.

In his obituary piece, Canberra journalist and former *Canberra Times* editor Jack Waterford described Lanigan's appointment to Social Security as a good move, writing that Lanigan was "an able administrator" who "oversaw important developments".[75] His description of Lanigan as a person, however, captured something of a man in a rush, at times less than particular about detail. Waterford also suggested the tensions, while working with Margaret Guilfoyle, probably were as much the result of his character as his interests – "a personality not afraid to mix it with journalists or take on all comers in debate in a bar".[76]

One memorable, and somewhat retold encounter between Guilfoyle and Lanigan involved his determination to make a senior appointment which Guilfoyle did not agree with – she did not believe the person he had suggested was right for the position. Rod Kemp, who says that Guilfoyle "didn't berate people, public servants, or anyone else, but she could change the atmosphere" (what Kemp describes as "a great natural authority") recalls Lanigan having it out with Guilfoyle in her office about his choice for the appointment.[77] Lanigan spoke on and on about his decision while Guilfoyle sat silent, maintaining complete composure. For all that, the atmosphere was electric. Kemp says it was if there were icicles on the ceiling. And on and on went Lanigan until, suddenly, he ended the conversation, saying, "I don't think I'll proceed with the appointment". As Kemp says, "You could never say that she vetoed the appointment ... but everyone knew exactly what she was thinking".[78]

The Greek pensions affair

Margaret Guilfoyle admitted later that she had always had reservations about the appointment of Patrick Lanigan to head up the Department of Social Security. Her intuition was to prove her right with the political fallout from what would become known as the Greek pensions affair.

On 31 March, the Federal Police, then known as the Commonwealth Police, began raids on the Greek community of inner Sydney. A few days later, the *Sydney Morning Herald'* carried a front page headline "Doctors held in alleged $6.5m racket" – a very large amount in 1978. Five doctors had been arrested, the article claimed, including three leading specialists. The charges? The doctors were believed to be part of a widespread scam among Sydney's Greek community to defraud the federal government. False medical documents had been issued as far back as 1971 to qualify members of the Greek community for invalid pensions, along with half a million dollars paid out in false Medibank claims.

The saga would go on for more than a decade but for Margaret Guilfoyle the most testing year was 1979. As the accused faced their fate and became entangled in a long and drawn-out court battle, it became clear the actions of the Federal Police had been excessively heavy handed and made in collusion with the head of the Social Security Department, Pat Lanigan. Accusations of a xenophobic targeting of the Greek community fueled attacks on Guilfoyle and the department by Labor senators. By early 1979, the Opposition was calling for an independent inquiry into the whole affair. There were accusations that – in spite of the Minister's denial that pensions of those not charged, albeit accused, were not to be stopped – cases continued to be reported of individuals losing payments. Labor Senator Arthur Gietzelt, in the Senate on 21 March 1979, accused the Minister of being unable to clarify difference between her advice and departmental realities:

> Mr Lanigan, the Director-General of the Department of Social Security, promised in a press release issued on 19 April last year that "no person need fear that he will be left without income". How does that compare with the statement of the Greek welfare officers who ... know that there is a vast difference between what has been said by officialdom and what has been practised in the field. ... There can be no doubt that Senator Guilfoyle has on a great number of questions failed to answer satisfactorily questions properly put to her in this place.

In addition to the contradictions about payments of pensions, the Labor Party honed in on the targeting of the Greek community. In February 1979, Guilfoyle visited the Primate of the Greek Orthodox Church in Australia, Archbishop Stylianos, to express her concern about any offence that may have been given to the Greek Australian community. Her press statement, after the visit, emphasised her concern and stressed her appreciation of the contribution the Greek community had made to Australia. The statement reiterated that the "Department of Social Security does not discriminate against any person seeking its services".[79] From Guilfoyle's perspective this was all true. But, as the investigations went on, the Greek pensions affair would unravel quite a few large steps outside the Minister's principled assurances.

Rod Kemp recalls Guilfoyle being forensic in examining advice that came to her from the department during the whole affair. "She was a very good politician," says Kemp. "I used to wonder at times why she was making such a fuss." During the Greek pensions issue, he says that at one stage "she insisted that the Director-General stay in her office and provide further advice on a minute he had given and he wasn't to leave her office until she got that advice".[80] In late 1979, the case began to fall apart when Chief Inspector Don Thomas who was involved in the arrests in April 1978 "gave evidence regarding the proposed reward to one informant, for whom a figure of $200,000 had been discussed and $30,000 agreed on well before the raids".[81] The informant, while being charged had been given a pardon. This then immediately gave rise to questions of how much the head of the Social Security Department had been involved.

In a heated session in the Senate on 14 November 1979, Guilfoyle deflected the charge that a visit by the head of Social Security to the Commonwealth Police offices at the time of the raids in any way suggested that the raids were made at the request of the Social Security Department. She emphasised the proper role of her department in seeking to prevent fraud of the Commonwealth:

> It is not the role of my department to determine when the police shall conduct raids or how the police shall conduct their investigations. It is the role of my department where there are doubts as to eligibility to see that these doubts are overcome. My department needed to have some direction on the matter ... That is the proper role of the department. If the police have stated that this placed them under pressure, it was pressure from the department to enable it to determine eligibility for pensions which it was continuing to pay. I would have assumed that if my department had continued to pay sums of the magnitude that were floated as being the abuse under the Act, without some consideration of this matter, it could well have been severely criticised.

Russell Schneider, who had worked as press secretary for Liberal Senator Reg Withers, concluded that Lanigan's appointment had more than a little to do with the manner of the Australian Federal Police (AFP) raids on the Greek community in Sydney and the intemperance of the outcomes. Lanigan, as Second Commissioner of Taxation, Schneider wrote, "was used to tough methods to deal with tough tax avoiders assisted by skillful lawyers".[82] Alan Carmody, as head of the Department of Prime Minister and Cabinet, had advised Fraser to appoint Lanigan to Social Security to get on top of benefits fraud. As for Guilfoyle's performance in the Senate, Schneider concluded that while skillful, it was also "at slight though not unstudied variance with the information she attributed to her departmental head".[83]

The case of the Greek pensions saga would have its resolution in June 1986 after a royal commission[84] appointed by the Hawke Labor Government had reported resulting in a payment of $10 million from the Commonwealth Government to 500 members of the Greek community in compensation. In the end, after drawn out legal appearance that cost so many so much, just one medical practitioner would be convicted, 23 convicted on minor irregularities, eight fined and 25 given good behaviour bonds.[85]

The Fraser Government escaped relatively well, however, partly as a result of Guilfoyle's ability to handle Opposition attacks. At no stage did the Opposition call for the Minister's resignation and, in the community, at a time of general cutbacks, the idea of pension fraud of any kind left a reasonable amount of sympathy for the government. Even the Labor Opposition accepted that there had been widespread fraud of benefits in general. Labor Senator Grimes, in the Senate on 21 March 1978, accepted that

"1977-78 was Compol's [Commonwealth Police] year for success". He had gone on to say with approval: "During the year major investigations involving many millions of dollars were undertaken and brought to the stage of legal proceedings." Jack Waterford, who knew Pat Lanigan well, believes that in one sense the over excited handling of the affair went back to Lanigan – "it accorded with his beliefs and prejudices, as well as his penchant for swift and decisive action".[86] But Waterford lays most of the blame at the feet of the then Commonwealth Police – "not a happy nor very competent shop". In Waterford's view, Compol's handling of the case was "a superficial investigation, jumping to conclusions, serious lacuna in the evidence, overstatement of the case" and more besides.[87]

Australia's chief accountant

The now iconic television series *Yes Minister* made its debut on the BBC in early 1980. Before long, Australians were watching it as well - on the ABC. Margaret Reid remembers the show was Margaret Guilfoyle's favourite and she could not bear to miss it when it came on during a working week. So much so, that Guilfoyle would have their committee meeting start five minutes late, leaving time to get to the committee room after it had ended. These were days before sophisticated recording devices, much less "On Demand" with Foxtel.

Anyone who has worked around a parliament under the Westminster system cannot fail to appreciate how cleverly and amusingly the *Yes Minister* – and later *Yes Prime Minister* – series exposes the powerplays of parliamentary politics. As Minister for Finance, appointed after the October 1980 federal election, Guilfoyle would have enjoyed its nuances even more.

The Department of Finance is the little sibling of Treasury. For all that, its role is a big one in keeping track of government expenditure. Guilfoyle was thrust into the job at a time of unease within the Coalition that all was not going to plan in the area of curtailing public expenditure. Inflation ate up any sort of income tax relief while impoverishing many on fixed incomes. As wages rose, wage earners moved into higher tax brackets so that a wage rise could be lost in tax. Even family allowances were beginning to get whittled away by inflation. In late 1980, columnist Anne Summers referred to family allowances as "now... a mere token monthly payment to mothers".[88] She went on to praise the Fraser Government for doubling welfare spending but then criticised it for not advertising this widely. "[N]o one in the government has been anxious to advertise the fact and incur the wrath of the 'small government' business lobby," wrote Summers.[89]

Malcolm Fraser was shocked at losing so many seats at the October 1980 election. In John Howard's own words, looking back, Fraser should not have been shocked: "The

1977 result simply reflected the unwillingness of the electorate to seriously contemplate Whitlam again. Once Whitlam had gone, things were bound to return to a more normal political situation."[90] Labor's new leader Bill Hayden had helped the party win seats, suggesting sections of the electorate were tiring of waiting for Fraser's promises to arrive. Hardliners on free market reform (otherwise known as the 'dries') in the Liberal Party room like John Hyde, Murray Sainsbury, Jim Carlton, Ross McLean and Peter Shack believed there was a lack of will by the Prime Minister to make tough decisions. Meanwhile, John Howard as Treasurer would have an impossible battle over introducing indirect taxation.

In her Keynote address to the Australian Womenspeak Conference in 2003, Guilfoyle commented on her appointment as Finance Minister in 1980 in a wry way:

> Perhaps because I was the largest-spending minister and perhaps unhelpful, in 1980 the Prime Minister thought I should be the Minister for Finance and stop all the other ministers spending money. One thing I learnt, particularly as Minister for Finance, is that ministers are all "wets" as far as expenditure for themselves is concerned; there are no "dry" ministers.[91]

Fraser now realised his years at the helm had not delivered the small government and tax reforms he had promised ordinary wage earners. Welfare had blossomed while take-home pay packets seemed not to stretch to the degree people had been promised. As Minister for Finance, Guilfoyle now found herself a gate keeper for Ministers and their funding requests at a time when the electorate wanted more for less. She would later say she thought of herself as 'Australia's chief accountant'.[92] To achieve smaller government, Fraser appointed a so-called 'Razor Gang' or what was in fact a ministerial Review of Commonwealth Functions, comprising Treasurer John Howard, Minister for Industrial Relations Ian Viner, Minister for Primary Industry Peter Nixon, Minister for Industry and Commerce Phillip Lynch (Chair) and Margaret Guilfoyle.

Given the reluctance of Fraser to countenance any real reform that might lose votes, the task given the Razor Gang would seem monumental. As John Howard has recorded, they were given just a few months to come up with options to both save expenditure to make possible significant income tax relief. He began working on schemes to pay for income tax cuts by introducing indirect taxation. Yet, even as the Treasurer enjoyed his family holiday over the Christmas break, Fraser had gone on radio to end suggestions there might be any attempt to bring in an indirect tax since the amount the government would need to raise from a tax on goods and services in order to fund real cuts in income tax would only push up inflation.[93]

Other financial reform ideas met with resistance from Prime Minister Fraser as well – ideas such as the privatisation of government enterprises like government owned airlines or the Commonwealth Bank. An old fashioned conservative, Fraser had no spine for rocking the status quo. So, now it was up to Guilfoyle to oversee budgetary cuts in individual ministers' portfolios that would not prove too unpopular, in order to finance income tax cuts to satisfy wage and salary earners. Added to that, once again, Guilfoyle persuaded Fraser to guarantee there would be no cuts to welfare outlays. You did not need to be Alice in Wonderland to find the task beyond the possible.

In her Womenspeak Conference speech, Margaret Guilfoyle admitted her years as Minister for Finance were "very enlightening". She sat in on every Cabinet committee dealing with economic matters and the security of the nation. She was responsible for the accountability of government. At the end of 1981, the Prime Minister gave Guilfoyle the task of interviewing all ministers on their Budget submissions before they went to the Expenditure Review Committee chaired by the Treasurer.

This may have been something Guilfoyle had suggested herself, in her attempt to find savings. Or, as John Howard would put it, in "dealing with Budget bids".[94] As she told the *Women, Power and Politics Conference* in Adelaide on 10 October 1994, as Social Security minister she had found it very helpful to have upfront advice from the Finance Department: "Finance would say to my department, 'Don't even look at that. We have looked at it to save funds. It won't get up so leave it alone' ".[95] She also spoke of her belief that the Department of Finance had people expert in many areas of government "to a quite detailed degree".[96] Her advice to ministers dealing with the Finance Department was to work closely with its operatives to get the sort of proposals Finance would approve.

Without real reform initiatives from the top, it was all any Finance Minister might do. Looked at from Guilfoyle's perspective this made sense. Looked at with the *Yes Minister /Yes Prime Minister* perspective it also smacked of *déjà vu* in the ways of old. Malcolm Fraser was more and more resembling a very tall Rt Hon Jim Hacker moving from one position to another without real conviction. Whether his Minister for Finance realised it or not.

The Razor Gang would end up being – in John Howard's words – a damp squib. He recalls having a major falling out with Malcolm Fraser over preparations for the 1982-3 Budget. On 17 June 1982, Margaret Guilfoyle announced figures that suggested a likely Budget blowout of around $950 million, saying, "expenditure during the year had been boosted by unanticipated wage and salary increases and some specific post-Budget decisions". In addition, the economy was facing a global downturn now known as the 1980s recession – unemployment would rise from 5.4 per cent in June 1981 to 10.3 per cent in May 1983.[97]

By the end of 1982, the Fraser years were looking nothing like the expectations imagined by British writer and commentator Paul Johnson, after a visit to Australia in the summer of 1976. Forecasting, with his foreigner's eyes, he saw a revitalised Australia after Whitlam and wrote:

> ... 1976 promises to be one of violent social unrest and conflict in Australia. Inflation, unemployment and tempers are high. Fraser clearly believes he must get the serious fighting over in his first year of office, before launching a boom on which he can drift to glory as another Menzies.[98]

By 1982, Malcolm Fraser was certainly drifting, but not on the waves of any boom. Over five years, four senior ministers had been forced to stand down – Lynch during the 1977 election; Withers after a finding in 1978 by a royal commission of impropriety in relation to the electoral system; and ministers Michael MacKellar and John Moore over the colour television customs issue in 1982.

Leadership rivalry had also broken out, destabilising party ranks. Andrew Peacock had resigned as Minister for Foreign Affairs in 1981, accusing Fraser of "great disloyalty"[99] and going on to challenge Fraser from the backbench in an unsuccessful leadership bid in 1982. As the March 1983 federal election loomed, during a drought with bush fires raging in south-eastern Australia, the Labor

Party replaced its leader Bill Hayden with the charismatic man-of-the-people Bob Hawke and within weeks had won government. Margaret Guilfoyle found herself on the Opposition Senate benches once more.

The Guilfoyle afterglow

In an interview with journalist Libby Lester a few years after she retired in 1987, Dame Margaret Guilfoyle reflected on losing government:

> It is very difficult to be in opposition after having been in government; it is difficult to find the role you are supposed to play. You are very aware that you have just been removed by the people. It gives you time to sit back and see why you were rejected, but I felt I had contributed all I could to the parliament by that time.[100]

With Andrew Peacock installed as the new leader of the Liberal Party after the 1983 defeat, Guilfoyle took the shadow position of spokesperson for finance and taxation. After the 1984 election she retired to the backbench until leaving the Senate at the 1987 election. Awarded a DBE in the New Years honours for 1980, Guilfoyle had always preferred to be known as senator. In retirement, she would be referred to as a "Dame". And she had become "as large a figure as you get in the Victorian party", says David Kemp.[101]

For some years after her retirement, Guilfoyle completed a law degree at university and accepted appointments to a number of committees and organisations including the Australian Children's Television Foundation, the Victorian State Opera, the Mental Health Research Institute, including as being a commissioner on the Human Rights Commission's inquiry into the rights of the mentally ill. From 1993 to 1995, she was president of the board of management of the Royal Melbourne Hospital. In 2001, she joined forces with former Victorian Labor premier Joan Kirner to campaign for more nominations of women on the honours lists. In 2005, she was awarded a Companion of the Order of Australia.

For all that, it was her role in seeking women to come forward for political careers in the Liberal Party – something she would never have countenanced as she herself set out in politics – that showed how far she had come in her life in politics. In 1993, Guilfoyle accepted the position of Chair of the Liberal Women's Candidates Forum – set up to encourage women to run for office as Liberal candidates. In Guilfoyle's view, it was one of John Hewson's finest contributions to modernising the Liberal Party at the time.[102] In the next three years, this forum and its many offshoots in the various states would make a mark on the Liberal Party's selection of female candidates leading up to John Howard's historic win at the federal polls in March 1996.

Given the job of overseeing an increase in women candidates, Guilfoyle rose to the occasion. A somewhat different message from her 1970s view that she wanted to be seen merely as one of a team, albeit a team of mainly men. Suddenly she could see herself as part of a sisterhood. As she told the *Women, Power and Politics Conference* in October 1994:

> On so many issues, as Dora Russell said, the women's voices were not heard, and she was talking 60 to 70 years ago. We are still talking about women's voices not being properly heard – they are still too quiet. And more women in parliament and as ministers will bring that change in the way that I think will be of benefit to the community as a whole.[103]

In the three years leading up to the 1996 federal election, the work done by the Liberal Women's Candidates Forum in getting women candidates into Liberal seats was outstanding. Guilfoyle credited the great work done by women like Chris McDiven whom she called "magnificent" as crucial. Guilfoyle praised McDiven for "the way she's supported and developed the program in New South Wales. More probably than any other state. If women are only one or two here and there in pre-selections, they're token and the odds are very much against you. You have to be absolutely outstanding or have the support already organised if you're not going to be numerically outnumbered".[104] After the 1996 federal election, Prime Minister John Howard was photographed with two long lines of female Coalition MPs – 25 in all – proudly announcing a new dawn for gender politics.

Yet Guilfoyle also noted that getting into parliament was one thing, but then women had to also get into Cabinet to make real change:

> Unless women are positioned in the Cabinet with that sort of responsibility, then the effect of more women in parliament may be felt in the parliamentary party but it will not be felt in policy development nor in implementation of policy in the same way that they would be if they were part of the ... Cabinet in which the decisions are taken and policy directions set.[105]

Legacy

In an interview with Margaret Guilfoyle in 1998 she opined that former Australian Democrats leader Cheryl Kernot, when she moved to the Labor Party, had no understanding of what it meant to be part of a major party. Kernot, she believed, was too used to a position where she managed easily with personality politics.[106] In the end, her inability to accept the direction of the party leadership left her adrift.

In a twenty-first century world of 24X7 media, social media and more besides, personality politics can be a temptation for those given a public role. This was never the Guilfoyle way. Loyalty and team effort came naturally to Margaret Guilfoyle. She fought her policy battles in Cabinet and in the party room – and she could mount a persuasive case. For all that, she never allowed personal disappointment to take precedence over professional performance.

In 1993, in spite of her backers, which included Victoria's Liberal Premier Jeff Kennett, believing she would have easily won the federal presidency of the Liberal Party, she had stood aside after pressure from her former leader Malcolm Fraser.[107] Guilfoyle respected Fraser's presence in the party and would not have wanted an unseemly spat. In the event, Fraser withdrew from the vote at the last minute when he realised he did not have the numbers and the position went to former Liberal MP Tony Staley.[108]

For Guilfoyle, politics was the party – not a personal crusade. Her contribution at all times was for the good she could effect and the chance to influence the direction of public policy. She respected the opportunities given her by the political party she had joined as a young woman. She accepted that it was not simply her ability and attributes that had given her the much acclaimed career she had enjoyed. Without the party, she would have had none of it. Her modesty is perhaps something sadly lacking in today's personality swamped public fora.

In the many obituaries for Margaret Guilfoyle, who died on the 45th anniversary of the sacking of the

Whitlam Government, writers spoke of her as a trailblazer for women. This was understandably true but in acknowledging Guilfoyle's greatest achievements, Treasurer Josh Frydenberg spoke more truly:

> If Dame Margaret's achievement was simply to pry open the doors of the Cabinet room then that in itself would be historically significant. But that is not the full story. Margaret Guilfoyle made her own mark as a minister in the Fraser Government and had a lasting influence on those she met. Every government of consequence has its mainstays – the pillars who are there through its entirety. Margaret Guilfoyle was one such pillar in the Fraser Government ... She was meticulous, authoritative, intellectually rigorous, calm, confident and no nonsense. She knew what she believed – but understood why.

NOTES

1   Author interview with Helen Williams AO, 25 May 2021.

2   Recording of interview of Dame Margaret Guilfoyle by Barry York, 30 Sept–1 Oct. 2009, POHP.

3   Author interview with The Hon Margaret Reid AO, 15 May 2021.

4   Author interview with Stan Guilfoyle, 27 May 2021.

5   Gerard Henderson, *Menzies' Child – The Liberal Party of Australia 1944-1994*, Allen & Unwin, Sydney, 1998, p. 284.

6   Robert G Menzies, Closing Address Albury Conference 16 December 1944 in Graeme Starr, (ed), *The Liberal Party of Australia: A Documentary History*, Drummond-Heinemann, Richmond, 1980, p. 82.

7   Author interview with Stan Guilfoyle, 27 May 2021.

8   Margaret Fitzherbert, *So Many Firsts – Liberal Women from Enid Lyons to The Turnbull Era*, Federation Press, Sydney, 2009, p. 72.

9   Recording of interview of Dame Margaret Guilfoyle by Barry York, 30 Sept–1 Oct. 2009, POHP

10   Terry Barnes, "There was nothing like this Dame", *The Spectator Australia*, 20 November 2020.

11   https://joshfrydenberg.com.au/latest-news/dame-margaret-guilfoyle/

12   Author interview with Stan Guilfoyle, 27 May 2021.

13   Fitzherbert, *So Many Firsts*, p. 73.

14   Author interview with Stan Guilfoyle, 27 May 2021.

15   John Larkin, "A Liberal Lady with open doors in her mind", *The Age*, 10 April 1970.

16   Author interview with The Hon David Kemp AC, 15 June 2021.

17   Malcolm Fraser in Hansard, Speech to the House of Representatives, 9 March 1971

18   Patrick Mullins, *Tiberius with a Telephone – the life and stories of William McMahon*, Scribe, Brunswick, 2018, pp. 389-390.

19   Recording of interview of Dame Margaret Guilfoyle by Barry York, 30 September–1 October 2009, POHP (access restricted).

20   Author interview with Kay Patterson 25 June 2021.

21   Author interview with Anne Marie Kemp 15 June 2021.

22   Rob Chalmers, *Inside the Canberra Press Gallery Life in The Wedding Cake of Old Parliament House*, ANU Press, Canberra, 2011, p. 89.

23   Ibid.

24   Author interview with The Hon Rod Kemp, 20 May 2021.

25   Ibid.

26   Ibid.

27   "Killen Guilfoyle sue", *Canberra Times*, 23 October 1976.

28   Author interview with Helen Williams AO, 25 May 2021.

29   *The Australian.* 6 November 1985.

30   Paul Kelly, *November 1975 – The Inside Story of Australia's Greatest Political Crisis*, Allen & Unwin, Sydney 1995, p. 239.

31   Ibid., p 240.

32   Anne Henderson, *Getting Even – Women MPs on Life, Power and Politics*, HarperCollins, Sydney, 1999, p. 146.

33   Michelle Grattan, "Guilfoyle's move rapped", *The Age 20 December 1975*

34   Margaret Guilfoyle, "Women, Parliament and Cabinet", *Canberra Bulletin of Public Administration*, No 78, August 1995, p 23.

35   John O'Mahony, "Gough Whitlam's Legacy – What Worked; What Didn't", *The Sydney Papers Online*, Issue 24.

36   Russell Schneider, *War Without Blood – Malcolm Fraser in*

Power, Angus & Robertson, Sydney ,1980, p. 38.

37 Michael Baume, "Business, Robbery, etc", *The Spectator Australia* 12 December 20220; Author interview with Michael Baume, 17 June 2021.

38 Author interview with Helen Williams AO, 25 May 2021.

39 Author interview with Anne Marie Kemp 15 June 2021.

40 Author interview with David Stanton AM, 1 June 2021.

41 Author interview with Andrew Podger AO, 18 May 2021.

42 Jacqueline Rees, "Guilfoyle: Australia's Iron Butterfly", *The Bulletin*, 24 January 1976.

43 Ibid.

44 Ibid.

45 Author interview with Andrew Podger AO, 18 May 2021.

46 Anne Summers, "Fraserism with a human face", *Australian Financial Review*, 24 October 1980.

47 "Profile", *The Australian*, 24 May 1980.

48 Ibid.

49 Schneider, *War Without Blood*, p. 153.

50 Author interview with David Stanton AM, 1 June 2021.

51 Author interview with The Hon Rod Kemp, 20 May 2021.

52 Ibid.

53 Author interview with The Hon Rod Kemp, 20 May 2021.

54 Author interview with The Hon John Howard, 16 June 2021.

55 Gerard Henderson, "Fraserism – Myths and Realities", *Quadrant*, June 1983, pp. 33-37.

56 Fitzherbert, *So Many Firsts*, p 100; Peter Bowers, "Guilfoyle's Victory", *Sydney Morning Herald*, 30 September 1978

57 Peter Bowers, "PM Chooses a Softer Option", *Sydney Morning Herald*, 1 June 1979.

58 Peter Bowers, "Guilfoyle's Victory", *Sydney Morning Herald*, 30 September 1978.

59   Ibid.

60   Schneider, *War Without Blood*, p. 40.

61   Fitzherbert, *So Many Firsts*, p. 101.

62   Ibid., p 102.

63   Brian Buckley, *Lynched*, Salzburg Publishing, Australia,1991, p. 114.

64   Recording of interview of Dame Margaret Guilfoyle by Barry York, 30 Sept–1 Oct. 2009, POHP.

65   Author interview with The Hon Rod Kemp, 20 May 2021.

66   Author interview with The Hon John Howard, 16 June 2021.

67   Author interview with The Hon Rod Kemp, 20 May 2021.

68   Author interview with Michael Baume, 17 June 2021.

69   Author interview with Marie Coleman AO, 31 May 2021.

70   Ibid.

71   Margaret Guilfoyle, "The Trailblazers: The First Women in Cabinet", *Papers on Parliament No 41*, June 2004.

72   Author interview with Marie Coleman AO, 31 May 2021.

73   Ibid.

74   https://adb.anu.edu.au/biography/lanigan-patrick-joseph-pat-25493

75   Jack Waterford, "An extraordinary life's journey", *The Canberra Times*, 7 October 1992.

76   Ibid.

77   Author interview with The Hon Rod Kemp, 20 May 2021.

78   Ibid.

79   https://parlinfo.aph.gov.au/parlInfo/search/display/display.w3p;query=Id%3A%22media%2Fpressrel%2FH-PR05003597a%22;srcl=sml

80   Author interview with The Hon Rod Kemp, 20 May 2021.

81   Schneider, *War Without Blood*, p. 153.

82   Ibid.

83   Ibid., p. 154.

84   Commission of Inquiry into the Compensation arising from the Social Security Conspiracy Prosecutions was appointed in 1984 and reported in 1986. It was chaired by Dame Roma Mitchell, former Judge of the Supreme Court of South Australia.

85   Anthony Nagy, "$10m payout to Greeks", *The Age*, 11 June 1986   *https://thestringer.com.au/april-1-1978-greek-migrants-unjustly-caricatured-as-welfare-fraudsters-12794#.YOUsS-gzZhE*

86   Jack Waterford, email to author 21 July 2021.

87   Ibid.

88   Anne Summers, "Fraserism with a human face", *Australian Financial Review*, 24 October 1980

89   Ibid.

90   John Howard, *Lazarus Rising: A personal and political autobiography*, HarperCollins, Sydney, 2010, p. 117.

91   Margaret Guilfoyle, "The Trailblazers: The First Women in Cabinet", *Papers on Parliament No 41*, June 2004.

92   Lester, Libby, *The Age*, 2 September 1990.

93   Howard, Lazarus Rising, p. 119.

94   Author interview with The Hon John Howard, 16 June 2021.

95   Margaret Guilfoyle, "Women, Parliament and Cabinet", *Canberra Bulletin of Public Administration*, No 78, August 1995, p. 24.

96   Ibid.

97   Ross Gittins, "The Lessons we have learned", *Sydney Morning Herald*, 5 December 2014.

98   Paul Johnson, "The lucky country coming unstuck", *The Bulletin*, 28 February 1976, p. 24.

99   Paul Kelly, "John Malcolm Fraser" in Michelle Grattan, (ed), *Australian Prime Ministers*, New Holland, Chatswood, 2000, pp. 374-5.

100 Libby Lester, *The Age*, 2 September 1990.

101 Author interview with The Hon David Kemp AC, 15 June 2021.

102 Henderson, *Getting Even*, p. 63.

103 Guilfoyle, "Women, Parliament and Cabinet", p. 24.

104 Anne Henderson, *Getting Even*, p. 65.

105 Guilfoyle, "Women, Parliament and Cabinet", p. 22.

106 Henderson, *Getting Even*, p. 16.

107 Michael Millett, "Guilfoyle gives in to Fraser pressure", *Sydney Morning Herald*, 6 August 1993.

108 David Kemp, email to author, 22 July 2021.

www.ingramcontent.com/pod-product-compliance
Lightning Source LLC
Chambersburg PA
CBHW060555100426
42742CB00013B/2562